THE GREY BETWEEN

POETRY BY

NADINE ELLIS

Copyright © 2025 Nadine Ellis.

Published in the United States by Hill of Content Publishing

Published in the United Kingdom by Hill of Content Publishing

Published in Australia by Hill of Content Publishing

Published in India by Hill of Content Publishing

hillofcontentpublishing.com

PO Box 24 East Melbourne 8002 Victoria Australia

All rights reserved. No part of this publication may be reproduced, stored in a retrieval system or transmitted in any form by any means without the prior permission of the copyright owner. Enquiries should be made to the publisher. Every effort has been made to ensure that this book is free from error or omissions. However, the Publisher, the Author, the Editor or their respective employees or agents, shall not accept responsibility for injury, loss or damage occasioned to any person acting or refraining from action as a result of material in this book whether or not such injury, loss or damage is in any way due to any negligent act or omission, breach of duty or default on the part of the Publisher, the Author, the Editor, or their respective employees or agents. The Author, the Publisher, the Editor and their respective employees or agents do not accept any responsibility for the actions of any person - actions which are related in any way to information contained in this book.

National Library of Australia Cataloguing-in-Publication data:

Author: Nadine Ellis

Title: The Grey Between

ISBN: 978-1-7637882-0-6

CONTENTS

Part I
SOMEWHERE BETWEEN

Not Looking For The Seeing	3
When Hope Appears	4
Where Fury Has No Hell	5
Beyond Quiescent	6
Lignum Vitae [wood of life]	7
Uncomfortable	8
The Woman Sits	9
Alter Idem [another self]	10
Another Self [alter idem]	11
Ex Vestigio	12
Child of The Inner War	13
Mister Doe	14
Red Ruinate	15
Blinman Boy	16
God's House	17
Waxing Grist	18
Returned Feelings	19
Mrs Raper's Dirge For Her Son	20
Mark of Little Word	21
The Babushka Recipe	22
The Killing of George	23
Disconnecting	24
When Searching	26
Post-Traumatic Stress	27
Wrenched Apart	28
The Perfumed Wars	29
Recycled Possum	30
Roomed In	31
As Conrad Sleeps	32

Mabel	33
Wine Talking	34
Multicoloured Possibilities	35
Enemy of The State	36
Women's Talk	37
Potato Love	38
Breathing In A Vacuum	39
Six Decades	40
Excavated Letters	41

Part II
THE WHITE

Instruction On ...	45
Expectation	46
Blind Deb	47
Bellbirds At 10:14am	48
Encased In	49
First Night In	50
Even The Ugly	51
On A Week	52
Consumption	53
Viscid	54
Wallacia	56
Sunday People	57
Koala Cuts	58
A Potter & His Wheel	59
Sneaking Out	60
Chopping Wood	61
Atmospheric Moisture Falling	62
Cone Treasures	63
The Mother's Pull	64
As Life Passes By	65
Empty Eyes	66
A Model Life	67
Conversations Between Hands	68
Sessions End	69
Solitary Confinement	70

Wake Early & Find	71
Under Sunlight	72
Highways	73
Seven Years of Broken Sleep	74
Jenny-Lee	75
Melding	76
Rehearsing Departures	77
Caustic Comments	78
Naha Island	80
Miscarried Away	81

Part III
THE BLACK

Rupture	85
Lifting Skirts	86
Out of Control	87
Karma	88
Redefined	89
Friday 13th	90
8:05, The Telephone Rings	92
Astrid's & Monty's Married Life	93
Captured Life	94
Family Trees	95
Brief Encounters	96
Call Girl	97
Redolent	98
Rapacious Farewells	99
A Mercy Bullet Killed	100
Anatomy As A Dance Student	101
John Kirwan, Died Aged 67	102
Letter To My Child	103
Maude's Holding Some Knots	104
Zinyachka	105
Chatte – Noire	106
Between Coffee	107
Burying The Dead	108
Your Photographic Title Read:	109

Deirdre; Eighty-Three	110
Hurtling	111
Passing Through	112
Asleep	113
Mourning – Before Time	114
Secrets Soaked In Wood	115
He Knew A Woman, Years Ago	116
Time Comes To Leave	117
Love-Dead Bouquet	118
Grounded For Life	119
Intensive Care	120
Her Stomach Breaks Out	121
For Better, For Worse	122
Us & Them	124
About Nadine Ellis	126
Connect with Nadine	127

To MB, KB, JB, VE, & BE

PART I

SOMEWHERE BETWEEN

Not Looking For The Seeing

Even with my eyes shut the white lightning turns
on fluorescent-tube wise across the black sky
of closed lids. Thunder's lightning as bright
as the tungsten lights I stared into
in my photographic youth – fascinated
by their strength, to semi-blindness now
that I should wear glasses, to see crispness
and walk without them when melancholy
envelopes me inside out.
What is this storm of hate I carry?

Is it the noise or what it represents, I fear?
This cacophony hitchcocks me back to that
trainwreck – not the stop, but the two seconds
after it all begins … the same two seconds
after the lightning claps its colour – I count
a child again, counting distance: *three thousand,
four thousand,* whack – and I'm ricocheted
against the metal walls, the blue emergency
bulbs spring on to screams I do not register
as the thunder of stones and pulverized wood
thrum the window past the glass into my head,
vibrate my bones – the same bass tone that sings
against my bedroom glass, now.

When Hope Appears
As The Darkest of Greys

You abound black gloss poured along dermal pores;
raven as nightfall, without stars to look upon
your summit, as morning air tinctures this death-sleep
dark drab. Unlit words fail you in this ebb
dressed in your black suit of sackcloth and ash.

Your pigment sulks its hue nine to five;
wherein the blackest route dark grey is full of hope,
but escapes you nonetheless as sand slips between
crevices, drawn by gravity to meld with earth.

You page the dictionary of strange animals
with craft harangued with dialogue from your depths
– this nadir of colourless paint drips pure;
you are an instrument of measurement:
an anemograph perceiving the force of wind,
a writer cognizant of life ... aching for a zenith.

here Fury Has No Hell

At my hub I hike the boulevard of broken,
wear smudge and pokey face as though I always did,
and wake detached, peel wounds back
to where in books black ink joins cell to cell

I scribe cathartic mores;
a woman's list of words I'd like to rub against my skin

and in the litany of sins read:
#1: ... the other *femme*;
#2: ... unspecified briskets ... and #3:
... delicate indiscretions that are not discrete.

Beyond Quiescent

Her armoured knight appears on a dream-wisp,
black-matte his shell – crisp as the morning dew
that bathes sleep to a porcelain face, as silk trails
the tears that pearl to his sculptured chest,
enamoured by a million nights of disturbed dreams,
long yearned, like the moon to a rippled beach
– pulls the tide closer as though no void exists
between the earth and self.

She chips the ice with the blunt edge – a knife
of unimportance, grabbed between thoughts
– smudged white, like words she never voiced,
and looks to where he lay – fluid in her arms
of world as she laps his edge like the emerald sea
kneading silica that one day will opalesce –
glass in window eyes hazeled in ardour,
leaking till her thirst is quenched

and until then, she scrapes the mustiness
against old blades of death, flicks shards of cold
that fall beyond the floor, and melt
into the unknown, as miles pass …
hoping the whispered musk of love
draws even quicker still.

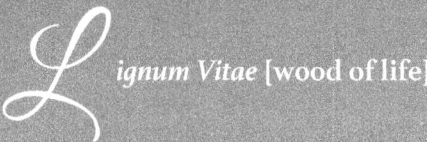

*L*ignum Vitae [wood of life]

He breathes *Latium*; offering words as water
rain-poured off leaves pulled to earth,
– feeds the earth, brown, lilts humus
as nitrogen from air changes to nitrates
that embody protein, that plants need
to grow, as children need love to be adult
in a world of unknowns.
He reads psalms
to be a vessel of words – monastery-practiced
in *literatim* where his only limit is flesh
and not cellulose pulp, but as *literati* he is
– as there is no *laudator temporis acti se puero*
only the present, and a chance to reflect
about the beauty ... of a tree grown.

Uncomfortable

We wedged into each other,
watching the flickering video,
pitted into the couch
like the dented pillows that lick our backs.
Not really watching as a family
but as a person and a person,
and a person, all gazing at the same
inanimate box, seeing different shades
of blue: cornflower, azure,
or even like yesterday's clear sky
when we shuffled home
to be alone, together.

My daughter dents herself
into my leg, I inch away,
her sudden heat bores into my thigh,
a throw back to childhood
where father's unpractised touch
wipes his thick palm across my back,
his misplaced gesture to tenderness
sends a shiver between shoulder blades,
my nostrils fill with his ammonia smell,
I inch away, again,
sinking deeper against the aqua wave.

he Woman Sits,

    her face toward joining walls
    should some stranger think
    to read her eyes, she guards
    her nape with wind-tossed hair,
lets pin-stripes deflect their gaze, down
    to sculptured legs, sealed shut.

    She rubs finger-grime against
    her china cup, glazed in
someone else's stains and drowns
    sweet desires, one by one,
as voices scrub the parquet-floor.

    The clinks exchange their cant
    for tarnished spoons dipped
    caffeine rich
and still her face chooses walls,
her nerve kept cup-sized, polite,
but caffeined-in, she sits – alone.

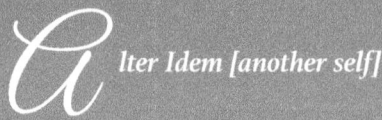

Alter Idem [another self]

Fugit irreparabile tempus in distans
sicut sequitur ut fulgurat,
desperatum,
cupitum,
delectatum ...
facile princeps
at spes non fracta
in esse
ex uno disce omnes;
clarior ex tenebris
... aude sapere
auctor pretiosa facit.

Another Self [alter idem]

Irrecoverable time flies on at a distance
just as it follows that there is lightning
there is despair,
there is desire,
there is delight ...
all do not look alike
but hope is not broken
in existence
from one of them learn about them all;
the brighter from the darkness
... dare to know
the giver makes the gifts precious.

 *x Vestigio*

I peeled back onion-skin off his mortal shell
as he acquiesced this nourishment; imperfect
as his hold on life dripped atrophy
and then awash; rolled clockwise
against perspex and lead ... baleful as once
when he returned home to possessions
in rain, but laughs now
as though that episode was someone else

and it is, and was ...

I splayed the crisp thinness out,
like an eggshell after birth is malleable
then hardens to the air; his fight now
is with self and what he should be,
just as dialogue about the essence of life ranks
number one; his conversation-need is balance
... between life and God.

# Child of The Inner War

Internal conflict is what she knows
like the Veteran who chases silence
but each night swims in colours of eternal death
– placated by white sheets that roll him back to youth,
but she was born into the year of nightmares,
and now each month bleeds the crimson of those
dreams.

And like the Honour Wall, cries poppy tears
that weep along the names that rise above the dead
– raised print that brailled bullets into bones
where salt will not hide the ammonia smell
or unwashed flesh, putrid hessian soaks this canvas.

But her war is with herself,
and these names are men she will never know,
they are the colour of dark chocolate
given over years ago by women
that suffered the birth-tables, bittersweet.

She sits like a wrinkled Buddha
weighted by the gravity of air, and for a few seconds
each day fights her conscience
to escape the razor blade prison of her skin.

Mister Doe,

born the year Sylvia Plath died,
bitter cold, so he suffers the ice-
mallet wedged between bones, and heart.
Dry-ice throbs that creep determined
willing life to greensticks, compounds,
that kissed gravel, made bitumen love.

And at fourteen he spread seeds
in an older garden,
only to watch his flower cut and carried
by another, so Mister Doe cut his manhood
and like a woman bleeds inside.
But he knows his limitations, rocks them
to sleep like mothers long after their child
has grown – rock, empty.

Now, maybe a grandfather at thirty-three,
his arms tell the stories his voice leaves out.
And as a woman's face shows the years
he also engraves his scars on the outside
to show what he's endured.
But unlike Sylvia, he'll persist and wear the cold.

ed Ruinate

I sit by the water hole, the Southern Cross
skred, thubs ... skred, thubs every revolution
as the trickle pees itself into the water trough
ten feet away. I've seen kangaroos drink there.
Their every shade reflecting rural tones;
bone-grey, tan-grey, grey-grey, their tails dent
deep the sandy dirt like bicycle-tyres criss-cross
a BMX track, the roos mark the spot,
among black balls of dung and splintered shafts
of air-dried cousins ... this is the outback.

A lone willy-wagtail deploys the deceptive
broken-wing dance to an audience of one.
Once when I was five mother said the willy
feigned her wounded frisk to draw assailants
away from the nest of eggs she laid.
But this is Autumn and the bird still jigs,
more in defiance, just like a few weeds,
the only real green not dead or eaten yet,
that dare to grow by the water trough's half-shade,
and all I can hear is its steady piss ...
and a blue dragonfly's *zing* as his yellow cellophane
wings reflect the sun, melting into red sand.

Blinman Boy
Flinders Rangers, South Australia

I sit in the corrugated shade
of the Blinman pub, deep in wood smell,
like old books touched by rain,
Pegleg Blinman walked the same slate,
laid his shepherd claim, coppered the street
in 1859, as I abide wrapped in this vacuum
quiet as though my ears were plugged
with his wool waiting a horse, or two,
to gallop past, make a noise, make any noise.
And the hill behind the dozen post boxes squats
watching both the post and pub ...

A hundred years is just a blink
an eyelash dropped ...

And when he'd drunk enough, he sold
his stock for 70, 000 pounds,
sprinkled the gravel with occasion
and now, with tourists, who wander down his street
and don't see the history, for all the flies.

# God's House

Peter traipsed across the slate doorstep,
entered the crumbling orthodox church,
air still thick with incense, like Easter
bakeries reek of cinnamon and spice.
The stain glass filtered blue and red,
instead of acting the priest's silent
fear of God, with the back wall smeared
with coloured strokes of Jesus and blood
and ghosts hiding the sacred men's room,
where ovaries never crossed.

Peter haggled the price for years, *a spur
of the moment* thing seeping into his skin
like christening oil crossed on Katherine.
But that year the Priest barred his wife,
said she'd waited more than forty days
to cleanse herself of blood. She swore
never to cross that church again.

Weeknights he shares the loft with pigeons,
sleeps on a bed of old pine pews,
Sundays, Peter shares with God.

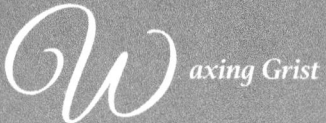axing Grist

One summer I studied
all four makeshift shelves
of mother's psychiatric texts
to be at thirteen self-assured,
while she studied psych-nursing
to learn she knew less.
I knew my boyfriends'
text-book motives, read them
one page-per-date,
their crisp sheets type-set
– psychiatry was my avenue.
And then,
one High School Spring I bowed
to fickle interactive needs,
ditched far too much school,
trashed my psychiatric dreams,
banished them to pleat my thoughts
in sleep, knocking twenty years
later at some Shrink's mahogany door.

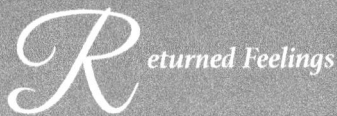eturned Feelings

Back when Rob and I dwelled together,
cohered in coexistence, we co-cooked,
and co-took the dog out for runs.
Rob trained her to race footpaths
alongside the Beetle we drove, fast,
I watched expressions as the dog pelted
through people, this mad dog
from nowhere, and then she'd whip
the corner as fast as she disappeared,
their faces popped with magic,
but with every trick hovers illusion,
behind the wheel Rob tugged alchemy strings.

And one day when Rob was caring for feelings
of mine, while I fluffed his after a quick wash,
somewhere, some feelings dropped,
and in the exchange, the dog lapped them up
to drizzle down some drain, eased to sea.
And I remember seeing someone else
wearing my feelings, once
when we co-took the dog for a run to the beach.

Mrs Raper's Dirge For Her Son

There is no liquid between us –
lapping my toes like a cat's tongue licks salt,
or sand to crust my flesh,
graze my thigh where your palm touches
like powder dusted across fingerprints,
or tomorrow where you trip
against the crevice in the deck,
mutter blue across your lips,
that will not kiss my neck – soft
as blood petals that you will not give,
raughty for shore leave. There is no water
in the glass smudged with your breath
that I hold to my mouth wanting
to breathe you in. You will not
knock on the door, rattle the hasps
as the padbolt releases its grip.
There are no tears to mitigate the sea,
as barrelled clouds ride time, spank water
in mockery. Those clouds siphon, as you loiter
on your molten sea, there, where you paint
HMS Sirius in melancholy, as travels
weight your brow with malaria winks,
that you will not fight in some sailor's fracas.

There is no liquid between us – just caustic rain
to cleat my dreams.

Mark of Little Word

He departs a train – on invisible lines
that each day draw him from this station
of thought, he takes our words
as though discarded rags – not intimate
wrappings of ourselves, we echo goodbye
as though it was the last.

He sticky tapes us back, when alone,
plastered along walls that line his room,
as though photos that stare him down are not enough.
And there, reads himself out to our flatness,
his words soak into crisp script that give us life.
He sits back in his room of papered self and waits,
for the exact predilection, the next locomotive
of locution, and dictates into dictaphones
of empty sentiment, as voiceless secretaries parry
to bring peppered breath to his life's sentence.

The Babushka Recipe

The children watched navel-dipped, one child per sink
soaking summer out of parched skin,
in concrete wash troughs, as she banged the dust
from Chinese rugs draped across the laundry line,
with the huge cane-key she slapped those ladies
delicate hours till their ghosts rose in puffs
and beads of sweat ash-smudged her cheeks.
And when her arms ached
she gathered children from the liquor
like vegetables for soup, nibbled their juicy bottoms,
blew bubble kisses into liquid-logged flesh.
In the kitchen she rolled onion bulbs under warm
water
like the washing of grazed knees, a skinned toe,
her fingers caressed crisp shell as she peeled
back thought, onion skin cleansed
like a fumbled truth – laid out wet,
cell against cell bound by her wrinkled brawn.

The Killing of George

Tube-stuck, a voodoo doll, he lies starched
on antiseptic sheets, his killing bed waits
like a tom stalks the hapless bird ... waits
... machines draw-back breath, his death-play
a part of life ... *Only the dying die a first time.*

As the youngling fallen from Spring's nest
grappled long gathering mini-beasts
to fester among its feathers like the ebb
and flow of maggots after death sighs.
The brown bird cried its bird cries
till George strode the path to the back shed,
shovel in hand and returned bird empty.
... I counted the ways:
One hand wrapping the body
the other ripping head from neck ...
A crunch of leather against snapped bones ...
The shovel smashing brains to mush ...
Tossed to the neighbour's cat ...
Or buried alive inside the shallow grave
of compost and worms ...

Who will raise their hand for George?
Who will turn the dial down, steal his breath?

Disconnecting

Removal first starts with mothers, then thumbs,
shuffled along by palpitating dental visits, scrape
plaque, and hairdressers to dislodge split ends,
while orthodontists chisel off cemented braces
with glared smiles, gas then yank wisdom teeth out.
You cram in *Moët* filled flutes strawberried with fruit
as a few babies rip out, compensating for things
disappeared, like the puppy, all those years ago,
people neglected to worm, who died painfully
along with that bit of heart cubicled for him.
But warts and dark growths burn unlike the foul
childhood taste of buckwheat-anything, that,
you can't remove. And then trying to convince
doctors that really you didn't want them to extract
your gallbladder, key-hole or not, forget the reach in
twist pull around to the other side tie in a knot pain,
you told them you'd watch what you ate – no
operation.

But ten years later, they cut, key-holed and some,
excavated the tumour ten centimetres and growing,
along with the fallopian tube it married.
And later still, time – disconnects; you watch twenty
minutes drift, the delicate crack beathing into
a zippered split of chicken sack and sodden chick,
then nothing, another ten and she spills out on
her back
– head heavy, wet, scrawny, her fork-tine legs poking
upright, splayed on her eggshell plate,
heaving for breath
... stunned at the quarried outside.

When Searching For A Woman,

glance below her wrist; check little things
like fingernails, digest each digit vision
without sentiment. Look for little bumps,
ridges, where layered lacquer hides altered
truth, splayed upon chipped keratin,
rough bits filed, then colour spliced
to match the stories she'll recite.
Spot the thumb-print edges of other nails,
imprints of her mark inflicted fresh
as last-minute polish-coats wrap around
the wheel of someone else's car.
She'll carry tardy varnish evidence,
like her motives, groomed at a hasty glance.
Note the line her nail tips take; convex
shovel-heads to gouge your heart, or blood-red
talons, grasp her prey, strip your flesh apart?
Then gaze the silken lover's thread wedged
between pedicured cuticles and skin …
if her toes bear paint, then she is beyond
your redemption.

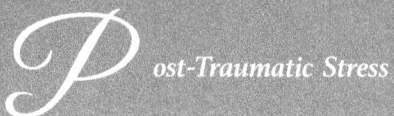ost-Traumatic Stress

Against the years of dreading planes
the Shrink delved and filleted
for weeks, bled her memory synapses,
squeezed drops grey, frozen, back
to the child, train-trapped, screaming.
With pressed-leg urgency
desperate to release a bladder load,
she'd closed herself in her coffin room
as railway stones sprayed opaque glass
like hail roaring on Winter nights.
Her carriage wrenched from twisted steel,
spirited at a 100 miles per hour,
though the seconds grasped her for life,
the train tilted, ground to earth,
smeared dust thick against flicked jolts
of blood dripping to the walls,
and like paper held in hands and crushed
between two palms, she rocked
useless in the bin. In her mind,
a glass of water remained
resting on the window ledge, shaken
back to place, never spilling the drops.

renched Apart

He wrapped his spindled fingers around her
narrow wrists, the tarantula tripping prey
within silk threads, spun from spinnerets
like blood pulsing to his groin.
She couldn't skirt the grime wedged beneath
those fingernails, seedling-beds turned,
beckoning Spring as he ground that soil to her
skin, mixed with spit as spider-hands burrowed
against the teeth of her jeans, her eyes scanned
the car as though separate from her head.
He pressed hirsute knees across her legs,
pinned her down – a picnic blanket, forced
to whiff his thick breath. He zoned in on her
freckled neck, drizzled slimy kisses across
her flesh – as venom paralyses prey,
enzymes dissolving her ...
And in his maleness mistook her
unfettered hand as liquefied, as it dived
to the floor searching blind; skimmed bottle-tops,
butts, then fingered cool chrome, just out of hand's
reach. She heaved a carp slapping body into air
against her water's depths, grappled closer
to the wrench, grasped its coldness in her palm
and whacked his throbbing temple ...
... the black widow tired of his mating attempts.

The Perfumed Wars

The black-draped tweedle-dumbs of men
dredge through maudlin life, murmur
their jaded mirth, ants searching minutiae
against chaotic death. One man, fatuous
as a skewed butterfly, holds his pants up
to the world, his only bunt-spit
to the common collective.
His stomach eats him, his words scream
inside his head. Only peerless dogs hear
his tones, whine sympathy to other men
who bumble late at night, trip
against their scented trails.
Grind love to a paste.
The jazzed moon cedes, assailed
by their cellophane bits that buzz, mere ants
scattered amid her nest as black scraps
trundle along the ground. Blind with eyes
these little men fall from heights
with a single touch of gentle flesh,
energy pressed to kiss the Royal knee,
she bends for her viands of automatic love.
Someone whispers: *She's been around some,
and in and out of that dress, you'd think
she'd colour change it by now.*
But only red will smooth harsh words.
And so, she sprays them,
leaves discarded corpses, behind.

Recycled Possum

One old boy steals finger-bruised fruit
    tossed in the upside world of black
to tempt him from the brittle conduits
    that zigzag like arteries pulse blood.
He runs the sun-bleached decks of night
    to search for food but scuttles home
each dusk to his burrow-box, until one
    bite too many zaps his possum bones.

His pliant muscles sizzle as smoke
    seeps to the lower floor, his soul
    osmosed in the allusive light.
Weeks brink, flow blue-bottled stench
as larvae mush the scrags, drop one
    by one from tiny cracks as maggots
steeple chase. Then the charcoal slate
    mutates to a boiling sea of ivory
scrubbed waves that swim without paws,
    suckled by possum meat.

Then the serried maggots exhaust
the larval war as they waft musk to sleep-
    sheath emerge, extend wire legs to black
    probe cold glass. Buzz-beating they wait
    to defile the next dead possum meal
that crosses the upside world to daylight.

Roomed In

The Daniel child shared bitter words
with his bedroom door, framed in pine
it kissed his cheeks good morning
or good night, as he crossed time zones
from their adult world to his angst.
And as he slept, stretched the generation
gap, woke determined to engrave
his rapid rise, one centimetre at a time,
date his mark, file the memories
that precede that height under 'L' for life.

His room, a hue of snuffed-out truffles,
breeds his contempt, and like fungi
sprouts strange things in the dark;
last week's pizza, three-day-old socks,
his body. The Daniel child stands girdled
within this outer womb of sustained breath.

s Conrad Sleeps

Mother slips wedded fingers between the door
and door-jamb, maybe Conrad dreams
of budded breasts, pouted lips,
his pubescent biceps scream shop bought tats
as he rolls in his boyish charms, wraps
his pillow-girl, kicks his head back, laughs.
Mother sees only hoods; flayed blue-grey arms
smudged deep within brawn, boys dated like her
youth, muscle tees ripped, Camel wedged
between cotton and collarbone.

Mother pined to smack lips on her neck
as sisters drilled hearts and lovers' names on flesh,
except Conrad plasters monsters on with spit, smiles,
knows it burrows under Mother's aging skin.
She sacrificed the tattoo boys to raise the kid
and sometimes longs for those men,
men with names etched deep as her furrowed lines,
but Conrad settles, eyes flicked with sleep,
and so, she turns her back on them ... shuts the door.

Mabel

Mabel Brown wraps wrinkled palms around
peach flesh. She smears ruptured fruit
against her wrist, lets the drops weep down.

Life-weary she stirs, a squark of cockatoos
scream past like white-paper reams trapped
by updraughts, corners flap endlessly
against the sightless wind as Mabel stares,
their name dementia-oozed.

Mabel Brown never throws fruit-stones away
she plants them all, her windowsill twig-full.
She says: ... *I never liked hugs,*
not even when Fred was around,
... thank God he's dead,
then sees another fruit bare its soul.

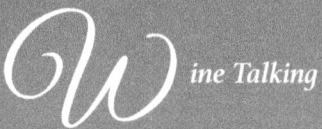ine Talking

Fruit borne from four crab-apple trees
breathes in the corner, watching us,
watching them.
Pink in clouded infancy and encircled
like the child within the pen,
the large onion-shaped glass balls
sing their bubble lullabies,
cradled, they exhale carbon gas.
And we, ringed by our small talk grow
tall with language as plants thrive
with the warmth of a few tender words
and a little touch.
Will the crab-apple wine drink stronger
when all our brabble is drunk?

One woman mists about the war
and how the crab-apple child
sings the squeeze back to her skin
with just a few little *plonk, plonk,
plonk* breaths.

And I look to the four bearing crab-apple trees
and see only shadows among them.

Multicoloured Possibilities

When I was a child, I dreamt in black and white,
zebra worlds where spoken words were washed
with shades of taupe and cream, and love filtered
through, the way coffee grinds flow
into the neglected Happy plant,
filtering its essence to the unkempt corner,
out to a liquid filled with heat.

When I was fourteen, I dreamt in red and death,
boy-men chasing my legs that slowed with each stride,
like the cartoons I studied weekends
in my foreign world of pink.
I lived that silver blade slashing my breath,
a balloon blown then released, my air escaped
with a hiss. I lay there, deep-crimson bleeding.

*Child-love, like rabbits die before our eyes
sometimes ...* I dreamt, or read
in some obscure pin-pricked angle of a book
to be at twenty-two movie-full
of multicoloured particles of life
that I breathed against those death men.

And now at thirty-three I contemplate
the purchase of two dwarf rabbits for my child,
to love ... and dream about in black and white.

Enemy of The State

The spider scutters across the limed-wall,
her eclectic walk oiled with despair,
searching a morsel to suck dry:
... Athena dagger-eyed Arachne,
taught her a lesson; left the maiden
wed-locked to web, forced to weave for life.
She plummets to the padbolt, brailles
the padlock with a plosive scramble,
free-falls to potato peel spooled
along the sandsoap-scrubbed table,
captures its fetid hessian smell.

The table suffers the spider
like the family that sit around its edge,
flesh growths kept apart by mahogany.
And as a candle burning itself out
the spider ripples an escape hooked
along the rim by a thwack of thick hands,
she falls a watercolour, backdropped
by dust, spills water-grey pear-drop blood.

Women's Talk

The deep self that has no name,
she said then rambled on
about façades we re-create
like papier-mâché,
one piece of news placed
upon another until
all meld unrecognizable,
the innermost starved, grey.
So the mirror-eyes dull the truth
and let us move in blindness.

And then she passed the bitterness
around and another
crinkled her little dreams across
the emptiness,
piled two sugars in and stirred.

 otato Love

She hunkers to the ground,
her heavy thighs mud splatter
as droplets dive one by one to soil.
She dips a callused palm,
wriggles a forefinger,
rough cold flesh touching hers.
Without thought she rips the root
to her chest as she might her child
pulled from his murky bath;

gathers him within her skirts,
gently turns his body,
eyes his eyes – brown, full of life,
full of promise: a man,
and food, when she is old.
But the child lies sleeping,
burlap-swathed, too young
to work the field
and so she dips again, and again.
And again.

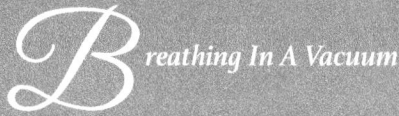
Breathing In A Vacuum

He paints scenes of words sable-dipped
– grey-scales that caress the crisp as monotones
of black and white – press lips to their page.
He trips across the path of her emptiness
and expands a world where she suspends
all thought, realities, feels nothing
but the heart that beats before her eyes.
A character he dreamed of in his sleep,
she becomes that which is splayed across
a screen, draped crimson and as plush
as velvet, dripped in blood, or saved
for another night, or knight that never comes.
Breathing in a vacuum, she waits
... for another realm, that he will write.

Six Decades

My skin is a desert –
not to be confused with desserts – says Wiki;
arid, dry flakes ... imprints
of the Kalahari, Sahara –
these are so beautiful when spoken,
a voluptuous woman –
created by the tongue
interacting against teeth, and mouth –
but my forearms are so itchy.

I'm not sure if I like the relief
from my nails scraping against the scales,
powering dusty DNA to fly
free ...
a sweet lilt of icing sugar – dusted
and gravity drawn to settle against the earth;
or the noise of keratin filing across
dermal layers – grating years off my limbs.

Either way, Verlet doesn't like that sound,
and lets me know I'm doing it, again,
each time ... unknowingly ...
like Lady Macbeth wanting the red gone
... I sweep the sands of time, away.

xcavated Letters

She once wrote about renovation
where renewal dressed a woman in cloth
remade of ardour, and he replied
exhuming her change as an archaeologist
pining long lost architects; not knowing
names for those who dig in ruins,
to him her *adagio* of cupped flesh to adobes
is a music cue, but he forgets she once danced,
and he wants to exchange his cement to mortar
but she thinks *Morte* is too close to death.

She writes letters because he lives in a world
of words, ephemeral as a stroke of ink
to the whiteness of a page; she builds colour
where there is none ... as he sees none
where there is ... and sometimes reads more
than she meant to say, or knows the whispers
that echo off his bricks, belong to her.

And like some Freudian test determines
who she is by how she archives a walk
around a wall, she formulates
that what makes a person is not written
in a book, but is read with the fingers,
brailed with touch.

PART II

THE WHITE

Instruction On ...

... A gentle balance
required like life, with body
weight centred over the centre
of the bike, and wheels like legs
work better paired.
Someone scratched underneath;
Watch the chain's teeth
they bite, like a dog
too close.
And textered over bullet-spits
in big black curves
an even smaller person wrote
about moving on,
and ... *never slipping*
on what had come before.
And to that end
I carved my questions.

xpectation

The clock breathes its slow click
as the light whispers to the window,
kisses the dusty ledge where her hand brushed
trails days before, printing fingers to the mirror
like the cyclamen that closes its petals to the night,
and in that red beat – the music of her sleep lulls
this emptiness back into the snapshot
that rests silent, waiting by her palm.

She is the paper – cut, cold, without the warmth
of sleeping breath to hover close to ripe lips
that want to press passion like a graphite smudge
on her whiteness, clean, without utterance,
her voice turned inwards like the words
one reads between thoughts.

She is tomorrow, where the stir of birds pour
their voices into empty bunks, as water laps a glass
to cascade – into the unknown oesophagus.

lind Deb

Deb wrapped body around cold-milk eyes.
Her under-skin pulsed rubies, sapphires,
her hair-waft rich in green apples,
and when she brushed by
her alabaster flesh hung heavy soap smells
like hand-washed lingerie fresh off the line.

Piano fingers played a person's face,
she'd shake hands by running chords
along cheekbones and lips.
Read a person's story through a brailled frown
and knew a liar by the dip in his voice.

Blind Deb faced ears instead of eyes,
rocked her head like felt-covered cows
that bobbed on teenage dashboards,
and shook all over when she laughed.

But Deb never spilt her milk-tears,
or knew the colour ... black.

ellbirds At 10:14am

These birds chime C, B-flat, C – tuning
their orchestra with an occasional A,
and then nothing more but the singleness
of a clear sound, crisp as a new sheet
bellowed onto a beckoning bed
or white paper – still, in anticipation
of its ink. Their notes resound
among the melaleuca, ghost gums
and the slight rise of grassy hill
where trees have spared the acidity
of eucalyptus – where grass waits
in trepidation of scratchy blankets
and crumbs, the sun sings the same
melody, lets little blue kisses grow
between the twigs and shards of bark,
cornflower-blue with yellow centres,
tiny mirrors reflecting back sun, sky,
grass stars – glittering in day.
A hundred metres away the chuckle
of kookaburras vibrate through
the piccolo of bird song – they laugh
at my avian naiveté ... *fool* ... *fool*,
they echo, as the orchestra stand
before their maestros. These birds call
it as it is – they don't sing B's and C's
of nature, they cast disparages on us
and laugh ... *look* ... *look* ... *look fool* ... *look at you.*

Encased In

I crave to close your eyes with my fingertips
the way my mouth presses to your lips rehearsed
at night, dark in empty beds. My heart melts
its blood as your words pull my body
closer until there is no room between
as I feel your chest rise and fall
with each breath I take ...
hear your secrets whispered in return
when you kiss the way lovers kiss
millimetres apart but still feel the touch.
I close your eyes so that fear will not
lustre; flare deep where I know you hide
... your chosen words spill in haste
to drip desperation that edges truth,
uncensored you pull me closer still
... to you.

First Night In

I raced the clunky bus around the corner
where the cabs ranked and hailed a stranger,
we drove to my new old apartment, duly overpaid
the driver and fumbled for the single brass key
to open the door to a bed, stove, fold-out couch,
and fridge, TV, and … no key to the front door:
Oh my God, I've left it at work,
and so, I sat on that cold concrete slab
as the sky greyed and a bit of rain cried
along my cheeks, remembered at the back of my head
in some compartment filed: *Maybe Retained
in Emergency*, and whisked out her phone number
she gave in passing as we met to maybe catch a drink
when I settled into the new town and all,
but not thinking she meant it, didn't write it down,
but as it had only been less than an hour
her voice still floated crisp between synapses
and grey zones. *Hello*, some male on the other end
and so began … *You don't know me, but I'm new
in town and (Oh my God what was her name)
gave me this number and my key – I've left at work,
and I've not even seen the apartment yet /and /and …*
And so, I slept on their couch, after he let me in,
and she didn't come home till really late
… And I've forgotten her name again, and his,
but I always check my keys.

ven The Ugly

A single carp bursts its water home,
breathes the same air as the crow
perched alone, silent in the willow.

Gravity torn the carp pulls back,
rubs against its liquid-hand, glints
a scale with sun, paints a star
on his sea-blue sky,

a flower given back to eyes.

On A Week
In A Health Retreat

The walking wounded drift in like dust
from the broom of life – swept by fruit
and chlorophyll-greens, they sleepwalk
behind the pied-piper of dreams, fasting
for days on water and squeezed juice
medicinally drunk as they float on
inner promises of health, while the rest
stuff vegetables into open mouths
of reality – *feed me, I hunger.*
Outside, the delicate chimes of bellbirds
flitter between the bush that surrounds
this cornucopia of people – they sing
vitality ... *eat* ... *eat* ... *food is life*
with each press of breath, as I saunter
to Tai Chi to practise wholeness.

I eye two staff tucked in a corner
away from clients' minds – they banter
morning chit chat as she brandishes
her dukes with a smile and tosses
her voice into the ring: ... *Hey, don't
forget – I'm Croatian, I know how to fight*
and he returns an upper cut: *But do you
know how to kiss?* Then turns lilting
'Danny Boy' in his Irish twist, dusting
as he goes, practising his wholeness.

Consumption

A young woman, angular, two days short
of twenty-one, fingers the dimpled louvres
that shut her from the outside. Her body,
languors under house arrest, kept shackled
by her honour, behind sanatorium walls.

She succumbs to TB like water-soaked willow
thin as the slender fingers that ply its strands,
succumb to cane ribs. Her lungs, encased in bone
give over to *tubercle bacilli*, the cunning killer,
archaic as the baskets she weaves.

And later when she's fifty, she'll reminisce:
fumbling along the halls like a drunk
without balance; the nasty girl who gave a dozen
sour-sobs for her birthday; the visitors cowering
at the foot of her bed, lest she exhale death-drops
on them; and the constant filtered air.

And then, sometimes, stifled by life,
she'll escape to the outside, to get a breath.

*iscid*

With lavish intrigue for honey and its viscosity
I'd unfurl curtsies to the ballet clock and scamper
downstairs to the delectable honey shop, lined
with buckets of tenacious fluid; amber hued
aquariums filled with the exotic: *acacia,
leatherwood*, turn the little plastic handle,
release a ropy twirl of sugar heaven, roll
the thick mix of bee and flower in my mouth
like a vinaceous swirl of Merlot to a gentleman
– a honey vigneron at eight.
And then peddle the half hour back, tripping
across Millers' yard to where lilting wax swelled
to two trolleys of hives parked along the boundary
fence – three boxes per flat top, with castor wheels
for manoeuvrability, or ease of distance.
I watched the confetti of bees wisp into their
compound
and feel their buzz wrap my skin, till my Mother's voice
out buzzed the bees calling me home.

Twenty-seven years pass and I smear cold pressed
sweetness across my toast, honey
that my Father extracted from Grandfather's hives
– hives I've never seen, but when the honey rubs
against my tongue I feel the paint flakes give way
to my fingers as I brush along the box and see
the bees panic as we puff the smoke
into their hexagonal lives, tricking their viscid wealth
from them in the haze of manufactured fire.
They fly blind to the truth, wanting to save
their vital fluids and then, collectively give over
what they made but was always never theirs.

And tomorrow, I hold my thumbnail to the horizon
and its width is hot fuchsia pink – a paint spill
bleeding out to burnished orange as the morning
rises to new flowers, and I will sup the pollen
from their flower pits and share the honey's essence
with the bees.

allacia

A housing development sprawled proudly
across one side of the road – boasting
U.S.-style rambling ranch gates
and olive-green oil-soaked wood fences
with kids barking at their dogs astride
the rungs like the horses they don't have.
We turn the corner from one treeless house
to find a paddock of leafless trees – branches
almost all pointing upwards tickling the sky,
and strung between each tree spider-spun
threads – silver clothes lines sparkling
in the morning mist and each tree strewn
with five to ten hungry webs pegged
to bare branches back lit by the rising sun
– a forest of lace doilies.
We turn and leave this strange America.

Sunday People

They walk the empty street
in recurrent silence –
a rehearsed wedding cortège
minus bride, minus groom,
remiss of forsaken friends,
just the endless vacuum
of the altar, and yesterday's
petals wedged against Cyprus,
the *speak now, forever
hold your peace* echoes
as a distant car alarm wails
to a void with no ears,
a crosswalk signal
activates with no one
to heed its beckoning voice,
only trapped green walk
to a programmed beat
... on ... on ... halt.
Sunday clan cross angular
paths to the afternoon,
cast shadows on vacated rooms,
scatter life-confetti
upon stoic streets,
as the crepuscule sun
touches grey and white alike,
anticipative
of Monday's cousinhood.

Koala Cuts

We swerved so as not to hit him,
a dog I first thought.
Without thinking we abandoned the car
as thieves disregard what cannot be stolen,
ran the ten meters to where we could
have robbed his life
and towered him like the eucalyptus
that towered us.
His eyes red rimmed as an old man
who speaks of his wife long passed
but still festering in his soul, glassy,
welled with tears.
And like my child I bent to comfort him.

And like my child he thrashed and arched
his back, more in defiance of things
he could not do, could not take the ten steps
without parental help.
In return gouged my flesh with two-inch claws,
shredded my kindness, scarred me for life
... as my children when they were born.

# *A* Potter & His Wheel

I have this picture of a man inside my head;
each night he undresses me unravelling myself

I am placed within his palms a miniature,
and on his clay wheel I spin, giddy,
as he moulds my shape anew,
a potter replicating himself through craft,
he touches with just enough thought to create
but also allows the clay to take its own form

with eyes closed, he knows I am water, silica,
and that he will emerge from his chrysalis
dusted with clay particles,
where upon he would look to a mirror and see
that he too was recreated ...

Sneaking Out

The clock's green light pierced dark air
like lasers searching the wall ahead
for escapees stealing into night,
second dots pulsed with each shallow breath,
as her shaky palms flattened against cool glass,
she eased the window gently, not to squeak
along wood rot and chipping paint,
sound parental alarms.
She pushed the flyscreen out, slipped into cold,
like a deep-sea diver cutting the depths,
a shiver ran her shoulder between the spine
and neck, she shook her arms, released
her better judgement, let it escape back to bed.
And waited her rendezvous pressed
among the prickly hedge like a prisoner
pressed against cocked guns might breathe
a last breath, and then a last breath.

Chopping Wood

The tommy-axe cold in my palm
flakes a few more speckled scales,
as I braille a thumb across Dad's 'W.G.'
on the butt, read it like a nervous twitch,
an offering ... the return, always the same:
Don't touch the blood chopper ... girl.

He'd take my hand in his massive palm,
lead me to the back shed
where the wood clumped, like wasted street-men
huddled beside the shelter-wall,
frost layered in beads of fear,
Back up girl he'd say, and swing.

And I wander the line of corrugated iron,
chipped and rusted as my memory,
rub the weary tomahawk,
as a snail foam-cracks underfoot, swings me
back but my grown palm stays empty,
buried under the hatchet.

Atmospheric Moisture Falling

Hypnotic blades splay the liquid out,
hug glass like old friends
as pressure squeezes the molecules
from drop to sheets of constant rain.
A beam of light escapes, spotlights
the stage below: Mac Trucks
in the giant's sand box, and like cards
cast across the poker table,
metal signs warn of labouring men,
but no work exists just past remnants,
rain tossed toys waiting by the roadside,
duped water crashing to its death.
With last breaths battered rain squelches
rhythmically, coerced by speed,
creeps upward across the screen
... trying to reach the sky.

Cone Treasures

The young girl runs among the sea of spent pine
cones, grey with sun's affection
but lacking now amidst Winter rain.
She grasps a beige umbrella,
cool metal wields white knuckles,
she holds it upside-down, earthbound,
gathering mud splatters.
Her pink cheeks bellow, content with pine
cone treasures and gentle rain,
rain that layers her skin like dew on cold daybreaks.

Then the wind steps in, reaches the pine trees
shoves them right, left, makes their green heads
embrace
old mates, loving friends.
She hears the trees creak, crack like whips
flicked into air, watches the pine-men shake
weathered hands, release their cones.
Her young fingers fish them out of her pine sea.
Her umbrella – the life-boat drifting,
the metal rod – a mast pointing the pinecones' leap,
and she … their saviour, the Lifeguard.

The Mother's Pull

A little girl adorned in crisp skin
so edible as an apple pulled from its tree
keeps secret its essence. Her flesh
naked, she slips into the living room;
a diver slicing water, no wave, no noise.

Her Linus-rug clutched with her left hand
the right thumb snug within her mouth,
releasing silent air bubbles to drift
invisible to her water's surface.

And then easing through her murky pool
breaststrokes to my chest and sinks
to my heartbeat. The way unripe-fruit
hides beneath its sheltering leaves.

She lies like a fitted branch to my trunk
... drowning to sleep.

s Life Passes By

The still state is what she prefers like the quiet
whiteness of snow, where everything is a snapshot
upturned from some old rust-pricked biscuit tin.

No more years of growths gouged from flesh,
scoured to make space for more fibrousness,
or diminutive death rehearsed during sleep
for final plays – tossed lines rolled
against sleepless nights.

But Spring comes as does old age
like some transient truth to perforate the ground
for new seeds to be sown. Her children rummage
the photographs that she tossed to one side –
all those years ago, trying to find answers
in musty-flavoured paper fixed with chemicals
that she cannot recall the names of ...
or why she looks so sad in those sepia tones.

# Empty Eyes

She's tossed against grimy vinyl
like discarded shoes, beyond respect,
as stale tobacco penetrates
the one nostril free of blood.
Tar-stained fingers print her
sweaty goose-flesh, then grasp
her slender limbs like chicken wings
wedged beneath roasted meat, held
down under the weight of four hairy knees.

Her eyes focus on the dust
smeared floor: scattered pull-tabs dance,
bottle tops bob between dead matches,
mangled butts, as grubby feet fight
for empty space, manoeuvre thick thighs.
Outside, a third pisses in the street,
She hears his muffled groans.
Then shivers her disgust
as saliva trails her porcelain cheek,
and foreign beads of sweat spill
one by one into her disbelief.

 Model Life

The white-tongue of fashion delivers
thudded primal beats: music tested,
marked to intoxicate.
The auditorium echo-soaked, beyond
the pine board barrier shelter pert girls,
slim lined and wrinkle free, like clothes
they're ironed flat, hung, adorned
by the woven fabrics of guilt, silver lies
and lacquered, with greed.

The mannequin world of flash and shutters
strobe-blue against the shadowed forms,
virginal boards raised knee height, wait
silent, their task to spring gently the heels
that tread upon the starkness.
But plastic wrapped catwalk-scrunch
of plodded model feet fade ash sprinkled
and leather scuffed in time.
So too the young grow wise.
But now, pinned, tucked, these girls
are coat-hangers – flesh *fatales*.

Conversations Between Hands

Discourse by fingers are how the deaf speak.
Each fingertip on the left hand, a vowel
combined with the right, paints like a tongue tips
teeth to form the sounds, resonate against the mouth,
drip concepts like drops of spit.
Hands gesture the words; force gives the tone,
body delivers the final blows, like fists-to-cuffs
slap sense into the senseless.

Sessions End

Hunched, over the pine table resembling
the rink, with its scratched surface
more from pen nibs, keys digging grain,
she reads the left behind names of lovers,
closes her eyes, runs fingertips across
peeling lacquer, her signature abrading
in the ice, she knows skate blades
from figure-skaters draw the lines.
She knows tomorrow – the ice is smooth.

Solitary Confinement

Faced with the outside – I choose the innerness
of folding calico and flannel, watch with intrigue
as minute death floats past my eyes – clouded
in life, each speck of sloughed skin witness
to countless touches, or brush asides.
Each tiny DNA robbed of breath, drowned
among the soapsuds like children
they will not become.

And those children will not hold me dear,
wrap their juicy flesh around my neck,
smell like the sun smacked against the towels
that flap in the breeze, or whisper orange
or frangipani in my ear, their breath – my breath.

I fold this sweetness over, and over
into neat squares and place the towelling
onto pine shelves. Ready for the day
the children do not need my laundry.

# Wake Early & Find

    My stretch of grey sand swooned
to porous rocks chipped and scattered
by the wind, softened by a strip of blue
  as a child would paint the sea, its kiss
    eased to earth and kissed again.
I walked atop a thousand-minute rocks
split and washed a thousand years ago,
  and saw jammed against two cockles,
   divorced by death, a dash of tarnished
    chrome keeping half a shell company
in loneliness. Leaping back to this brink
  as a wisp of demise pressed my face,
    I dance across the grey sand mislaid
    within someone else's acrylic dream.

nder Sunlight

He wakes to feel dust-pressed wings kiss
an eyelid, as she hovers – a Monarch tasting
flowerets; a seraph *ex amorem*
on mornings malady-dripped,
where whispers secrete from his pores
– from the tongue and lips imagined
in a dream, whisked from petal lairs,
until her sex touches him
and pollen thirst forges another nightfall,
nourishing his existence.

Highways

Bitumen caressed wheels swoosh
a love-dead bouquet, balanced upright
against the reflector post,
not unlike the thousand passed but unlike
for all the faded flowers this one holds.
As four crows waddle across the road,
old men, hands clasped behind backs,
black bellies high above feathered belts,
old friends they talk among themselves,
and the slabs of blow-outs, and splattered
animals, hit in the night. The old men
weave amid the giant witches' brooms
of trees buried naked trunk first, bereft
of leaves, branches held to the sky, child arms
stretched to its mother, waiting, waiting
for another hiding hole to grow legs,
reposition itself, never the same tarred road
... never the same journey travelled.

Seven Years of Broken Sleep

Each night a tiny foot, unborn to air, thrust
my ribs; pushed between lung and bone,
punched, wrapped hands around my bladder,
squeezed, as though searching a way to retreat.

In return, my eyes wedged open, dark forced
my mind to gush the day's events over, over,
over again, till my brain-movie was right.

Now I wear cracked nights like second skin,
glance the bathroom mirror, rack my mind
to recall what I looked like before I had kids.
Before my dreams oozed out my ears, melded
into the pillow that comforts my head,
like my mother's lap did when I was hip height.

And now darkness whispers its silence
as the night-time creatures begin their day,
innocently traversing the stairs, each child
taking her turn, ticket paid by unseen token.

Magnetically drawn to me
like the North arrow to its home.

Jenny-Lee

She sits at the kitchen table, raw, as rain
nails throw against the corrugated roof,
a churlish football crowd, voracious
in the opposition's goal ... she counts
every point – mud grained along
skinned knees of youth, turned terracotta
– the game plays children trip against,
notch into skin as scars to be counted
on dark days as this, or forty years on,
when she scans the cupboard bulging
cat food since 2020.

She fingers her blue-tinged metal frames
fragile as empty bone – sucked of its marrow,
and hides behind the glass, glazed rainbow,
worn for days when the rains don't fall,
or they fall only on the inside ... She recalls
lolloping at eighteen and umbrage leaking
from fingertips that grasped the first letter;
her birth mother lamenting the handing over
of an adopted child. But the hyphenated girl
thrives on hard, she sits in longanimity,
writes a letter back ... *I did this, to you.*

Melding

The ghost gum dapple touches my skin
like a bodiless finger, poking my leg
but all I feel is the sun's hum
along my left calf, while the other
stands a twin behind itself.

Planted on a cerulean bench, I wait
for the birds that argue out of sight,
hear their slaps and spits but only
see the limed-newness of leaves
not yet run across quiet beaks,
as shadow brushes gravel, like the birds
that tweak and scratch the air.

No one sees me here, I am the bricks
I block. The day star melts my skin
as I slip into parched cracks,
left only with ants to trace the outline
with their squiggles. To them,
I am the motionless gum,
dappling their ground, with darkness.

Rehearsing Departures

We huddled, rabbits awaiting the hunter's
blinding beam – snuffle a cotton-tail away,
spear warm flesh with searing heat,
but instead, I boarded the Indian Pacific
with one minute to paint your face to my eyes
– those same blue eyes that painted mine
to yours when you were born,
and how I wrenched my face then
as midwives tore you from your burrow.

And as you run along the platform hair sweeps
across your face – a curtain drawn apart
revealing *your* wrenching face fighting back
tears you haven't learnt to shed yet,
tears that will brew for dead animals
and unreturned love. But I see you
keeping pace with my train and I whisper
to the glass between us ... *don't leave me*
... *don't leave me.*

austic Comments

Back, when I wondered concrete-corridors
of green youth
I was stabbed in the butt with a protractor
Who does that? ... I asked myself, even now.
... Mean girls – grow to be mean women
... I still tell myself – about that episode
so long ago – it was a lifetime passed.

Back then, my teacher – to my face – acid etched:
"You'll never amount to anything" ...
at fourteen dripping her acrid words
thinking: ... *Why would Mrs Ursini say that?*
... I asked myself, even now. My flesh still scarred
with her pungent laser cuts,
and mordant attitudes ...

and all this sulphurous mud before I even knew
what neuro-spicey was ... and is. But now, I do.

And once,
he called me: "*a silver-tongued snake*"
... but what did he mean? I considered
in shame –
only later I understood he was projecting,
that was when I couldn't do what he demanded,
my belly already with child –
replicating him ... and my autism.

Looking back now, I comprehend,
my firstborn carries my spiced-defiance,
and I understand one must wade the quagmire
depths, weighted by tasks that grind us down
to emerge regenerated ... Phoenix
shaped by caustic malevolence, soaring, above.

 aha Island

In later years she searched the map,
placed her island as an outstretched tip
about midway between a full stop and comma
fallen from her country sentence.

The ice-blue peacocks, and albino hens,
with their flushed eyes like the pink-eyed
fruit bats that hung fruit-wrapped at dusk,
strutted wherever she walked,
and wherever she turned azure touched her
like unset agar-agar coating a layer of salt.

She'd never need to see that water again,
... it filtered to her heart. And later still,
when thinking about her auburn hair
no more than just a thought, captured
in even older photographs ... now replaced
with dreary faded-brown, and white;
how she's pulled to those wistful times
upon sand easing under foot, or pondering
water buffalo tilling rice fields she passed,
as the launch danced salty upon that blue
heading to Naha. And at that interval
she didn't know those last East China Sea
days – just being, would be her turning point.

iscarried Away

Gravity drawn globules oozing rubies,
these are weeping tears,
snail paced they etch blood trails.

Oxygen rich but without breath,
they pool then creep outward,
heavy – in infant death.

PART III

THE BLACK

Rupture

Old Mack's gramophone fractured the air
with skittish songs lilted along the breeze
as he pronged the worm-turned soil
with weathered graip between callused palms,
palms that long forgot the softness
of a woman's flushed touch
after tenderness, long lost fingerprints
that danced along his clenched hand,
but his caress is for the dung he lifts
between those four metal prongs.

The record jumps a chord, plays the old
refrain of youth as his guttural *haw haw* melds
with Mick from two farms North, they grabble
on all fours, smear the dust-ground floor
with sweat, play for sheep, and Mary.
But the rural ruse is real, and old Mack
swipes the millionth fly and churns his guts
trying to recall her downy face catching
glints of sun and he just can't think
what colour her eyes were, or why she left?

# Lifting Skirts

1

Daniel's bony fingers wrapped my wrist
as he whisked me behind Dad's shed,
like puppies we scurried between shrubs
and trees, then shunt against the backyard vines.
He tugged me down, cold
hard concrete flanked my legs, cold hard kisses
pressed my lips. This was slimy love, at eight.

2

She jerked, left leg jammed stiletto first
between the grids. Clipped as a chicken
with half a wing, her mind flapped
but she stood still, flicked her raven head down,
collected two grubby men with her eyes, eyeing her.

3

Roz sprawled across the chair, her face gilded
as a filigree against the light. She clung
to her tangled words, saddened with each
new clutch of tales. She rose to spindled legs
and lifted her skirt to the fire,
once more, to grope the fingertips of flame.

ut of Control

Vibrations tremble under foot, an echo
from next door, him bashing the timber shell
like a piece of steak, pounding his mallet
fist with each word as my heart jumps a beat.
My thoughts shriek of her purple skin
and crimson scattered clothes, crusted
as an eye-steak that's rolled with bread
crumbs, pan fried in saltless butter,
cold comfort to his heat.

Two minutes earlier, I craned my neck
hard right to watch her reflected
through my vanity mirror, watch her
cook his breakfast meat like the loving wife,
her whispered breath too heavy to hear.

While the outside glistens, water coated
by the early flush of a shopkeeper's hose.
And everywhere tired cigarette butts
squashed by smokers' feet and nicotine sucked,
left for the vagrant to peel and roll
between thumb and forefinger
like a pulmonary press for life, tumble down
the drain next to where the plastered fliers howl:
No smoking here, no making early death.
And instead of her, I cower
locked behind the bathroom door … and scream.

arma

Jack Mariner stands grey, salt chafed
in Winter's rain that melds with sea.
From the beach he watches light crack
the sky's page, centering indigo, ruling lines
for ships he sailed, laid lonely words upon.

Back when sleep stole time on board,
caressed in canvas; an embryo wrapped
within its womb, he dreamt Pacific
waters embraced in kelp, blue fingers
that kissed his skin just like paramours
he touched goodbye.

And only now, separated by the sand
that eases between cracks in his soles
can he reel off their names ... *Avarice*
his favourite always floating to the fore.

But shore-sleep alludes him,
on rusted springs he tosses against the nights.

edefined

She drew flavour from the air of night
– delineating the unseen cords
that compelled her truth to a piquancy
forgoed, however craved.
Then wiped those unclothed scars
that wept packages bent out of shape,
as she watched her tepid death treacle
down cliques, poured cautiously hence
time would not assume to change,
where she bared past to the old,
and mystery to the unprepared.
While incongruity grieved, adhered
to integument, pared without valour
as another lingered potent
in the pedigree. She sought arias,
whispered to bathe that desire,
caress her outer-ness, as she
internally longed to hear him breathe
… and breathe …

# Friday 13th

Friday thirteenth stumbled in
as Mother pulled her teeth out,
wrenched and twisted –
she loved to gnarl a bone
but her white dominos scattered
atop the sterile Dentist's tray,
laid to rest among his archaic tools.
– her hand played.
And I ask: *How old is Mother now?*
... calculate to middle age,
a number beyond my memory,
and think back to the time I trekked
from Cradle Mountain to Lake St. Clair;
stole nature with my eyes,
I drank from iced mountain streams,
kissed water-falls with my fingertips
– water the tinge of Mother's tea,
more from the Button Grass tannin
than Lipton. I even felt the nip
from a leech feeding on my chest.

And all the time I walked those tracks,
one foot placed in front of the other,
the way she stepped off the ship
one foot in front, hand in hand
with *Tubercle Bacilli*
one breath in front of the other
or earlier still, 1939 – her first breath,
not once did I think about her
or the slow death that follows
the procession of fallen teeth,
tooth fairies depositing coin-thoughts
in trade, one tooth next to the other
... one headstone carefully placed.

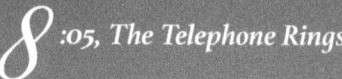:05, *The Telephone Rings*

Like icy water poured against the haze
of Winter baths, his shrill call steals her heat.
She skitters to the phone, as liquid
tumbles along her flesh, water-tongues
licking skin as they descend.
His voice spills out: *working late*, sends
a chill through the cord, scuttling
across her spine, prickling to her thighs,
her arms sweep the towel to her breasts.
Restless against the night she wanders out.
Distant car alarms wail, as a child would cry
abandoned to the dark. Her eyes,
like cross-walk lights flick on and on
... searching.
8:55, she sits where the corner meets the room
and sprawls her eyes across the thieves:
a lover snatching married time,
cascading lips, against *her* husband's flesh.

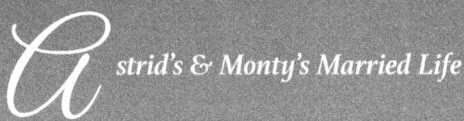

Astrid's & Monty's Married Life

Astrid flopped across the bed,
like a diver whose jump faltered.
He groaned as if she'd landed
on an imaginary cast, not yet set
or scribbled, then poked his mouth out
under the pillow, as a turtle tests the air
outside its shell.
Astrid flung slender arms above her head,
rolled to her stomach, smoothed ridges
in the flannel sheets, her palm flicked
mid-action, swept two hard crumbs off
the bed: ... *You've been eating again,
how can you sleep all night grinding toast?*

And in his mind he thought:
... better to pulverize the bread.

aptured Life

Like the rhythmic creak of wood on water
– but quicker than the lapping, she squeezed
within my world like germs beneath my nails,
to reappear weeks, years later
as the movie that flickers beyond reach,
or the book never completed, and I'm thrown
back to the lulling of flapped water across the hull,

back to the child woken bolt upright to lion-snores
that pummelled the bedroom walls, convinced
ghosts banged the door.

I turn the page.

Years later, the liquid song underlies the weep
for reprieve as my husband gives rise
to visits with the door-ghost. And in that flash
of flare-gun I fall to the deck –
like the fallopian tube left on the operating floor
as white coats gouged the tumour that grew
bigger than a baby's head. I carry scars.

But her words are scabs to pick at, nudge me
over the edge, leave me bleeding more than red.

amily Trees

Valencia's tree, planted in the May earth
the year her mother bore her branch
with a husband who knew alkalinity
of soils and castings not childbirth.
A sapling she watched maggies rake leaves
with claws, like her, rummaging Autumn
with toes searching tomorrow,
as she orange-blossomed before their eyes.

When the first gnarled knots grew deep,
green bulbs sprouted like pimples on her
teenage skin, erupted to green balls oranged
by sun, caressed by the pitching wind.
Her Winter oranges grew from branches
thick as her arms and thighs, held by pith,
as old as the girl, but each year anew
with fingertips grasping heroic fruit.

And one Summer when honey lilted
thick over air, the year she carved a heart
for the tree and tasted the bittersweet flesh
of truth as her garden father dug up her
mother's roots, ring-barked his wife.
Valencia counted the days till Winter brought
the inevitability of rain, and oranges, again.

rief Encounters

The front, covers the 'Court of Trial',
dated 'Sessions', complete
with 'Particulars of Offence':
Sexual intercourse without consent.
The Prosecutor's yellow tags
are pressed to crisp white pages,
like the accused was to the girl,
a list of names cascade, prepared
for Court; memory joggers, every piece
of inch-long tag depicts where
the next account begins. Witness lists,
points of view shaping one story
with each statement, thick with words,
double spaced truth, lies.
The top of the 'Brief' in bold print reads:
COPYRIGHT RESERVED ...
And so, the judgment begins.

 all Girl

Cornered by a lumpy man and walls
she brailled chipped paint across her palms
as his pub smell stained her fear,
like gloves wrapped around thick hands
pig-skin soft but tough, she uncurled
the whisper of black along her English leg.
The other still pooled at her glossy toes,
she fingered crumpled bills shoved
between her bra, ran a fingerprint across
the lace holes, grabbed his eyes
with her breasts, as a hand grasps an axe
takes control. But his thick thumb danced
against her neck, plunged into skin,
made blue pulse across her face,
drew dark crimson from her soul
as her finger-braille now scratched
his lumpiness, horror oozed from welts
she gouged in his flesh, as she breathed
one last breath ... one last breath.

edolent

Twenty meters on, the old guest home ruptures
its stones late at night, when even the wedgetails
won't hear the old men's stories spilled
into the rubble pile or the *one last bottle before
I goes back to me homestead* and that same old
cracked face that stares back, those thick bottles
lay embedded, shattered like men's dreams,
black as coal, the bottle slag pile's whispered truth.

Down the road, some forty odd Ks, someone
pine-ribbed chicken wire then mud filled the gaps
to make walls, and a roof of corrugated iron
like the corrugated track walked to this home,
the floor packed hard, stamped, stepped again.
Only carefully laid stones still shape the fireplace,
that burned the leftover pine, kept warm
in this cold house, where the children were born,
bore chicken pox, pneumonia or easier still ... death.

But the Ranges still cast a pink glaze among
million-odd old shale, rock, as the breeze lifts,
turns barbed wire on to razor wind, buzz-humming
morse: *night comes, night comes,* and so do the young,
their dust trails ribboned behind 4-wheel drives
... and like the dead, they'll also pray
for an inch of rain at the end of the month.

Rapacious Farewells

When you trample the dry-wash of rolled stones
and tree-bones deceived by soil, fractured
by the gush rained hours before, miles beyond,
years ago – picture those given over to water,
faces wrought by abrupt cold smacked across
flushed skin.

Listen, you can hear a magpie's warble cleave
the creek-bed. She sings the dead men's last clutch
laced by a drift of screams – not the slow formality
of rasped breath from a feeble chest,
as splenetic growths expand in months ahead
– but lungs that heave to push death out.

The brisk seize of air scraped against those throats
as water surged faster than fear giddied their flesh.
Walk the dry-wash rim for those who cannot walk
on water, listen carefully – you'll hear their wheeze.

A Mercy Bullet Killed The Electrocuted Possum

A cumbrous ball of sickness wedged
between my fortitude and gut, twisting
my tongue with an adrenaline tang
as it sat behind my throat, waited
one more visual overload from retina
to brain, forced my clammy palm to mask
the up-chuck as I ran the sponge along
the rubied lines, pressed the blood in
upward strokes as water-diffused colour
ran the pine walls, like cordial spilt
on cloth – stains cloth, blood stains wood.

Globules oozed from cracks upstairs,
ended as the ceiling above, warm death
treacled down then splattered red.
I scrubbed in haste, avoiding young eyes,
till only the air remained rank
with burnt flesh. But how can two retinas
be scrubbed from the inside?

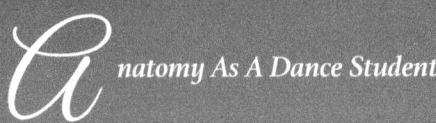natomy As A Dance Student

I still see them in neat rows, laid on chrome,
snooker tables, lined on body-width by body,
my marinade men leap up at midnight, *pirouette*,
play ball when medical students depart.
Do you miss my scalpel flesh-stripping your back?
I released globules of yellow fat, clumped where
the tissue no longer bleeds, and my horror
at sixteen learning the fundamentals of Anatomy
one-on-one, on death left for science.
And I miss the sinus-stripping indescribable stench,
formaldehyde seeping into every pore of walking flesh
and I peel back their white modesty cloth, dissect
muscle from scapula and try to memorize
muscle names but all I cannot forget
is the one silver tray beside my gurney, asserting
its assorted penises, attached to shrivelled pouches
of emptiness lined one-by-one, a mini version
of the morgue, this is what walks out that door
... this is what I cannot forget.

John Kirwan, Died Aged 67

Just a grey slate headstone, its back
facing the sun and leeward John Kirwan,
from Ireland, facing nothing.
The stone mason carved him well:
January 1, 1873 ...
In Memoriam ... but the rumour
still lingers, poor John shot himself
in the head; the damn fly entered his ear
and drove him spare, and so he did
what any other man would do,
given where he was and all ...
So, they buried him near Edeawie Gorge,
but still not far enough, to get away.

# *Letter To My Child*

Your body unfurls from the inside – dehiscent
a flower burdened by fragrant petals ... fastened
with torment, and heartbreak-laced – aching to bloom
Helianthus, as *H. annuus* ...
my amber-rayed Sunflower – awaiting
your transition, realignment ... efflorescence.

Maude's Holding Some Knots

Maude lingers in the bedroom dripping memories,
draped by faded black and whites;
a man wrapped in chiselled skin, *Robert,
my brother*, she thinks, but it's really Ted
the day before he cherished her, a bride.

And Maude's daughter explains dementia
to her child: *as if memory were a piece of string,
held between the left palm and the right.
Hungry, dementia eats the short-term memories
held in the left hand, devouring towards
the long-term grasped within the right.
... All the way back ... Everything.*

She keeps that bedroom spotless, no creases
on covers, lays the jewels out, waiting
for the lady, waiting, in case she comes back.

inyachka

She sat engulfed by her red-room.
Age laden, as always she pulsed tobacco breath,
crepe-papered her skin more each day,
and crocheted her mustard-yellow cape,
that carried holes for my childhood
finger-worms to weave, in and out.

All her finger-tugs at plush-life draped velvet
among her shrivelled legs. Every drag of fabric
pulled along cracked eggshell nails, scratching
for scissors as chickens scratch for worms.

And as a child she crept marble stairs
to feed Jews her beetroot soup.

And I watched her fingertips, egg yolk dipped,
stained in nicotine, each delicious
against tobacco meals she smoked instead of ate.
Never far those cigarettes, clutched
like children sheltered from howling bombs,
she hid her leafy-brood tucked tight beneath
crocheted wings, roll called them one by one,
each crisp shell wrapped in death.

And then one day she struck the final light,
rattled deep her velvet breath,
savoured the last red-room cigarette.

hatte – Noire

This is the black cat that doesn't cross the road,
laid out on the footpath sun basking in death
with a slow final shit-tube panic pressed
– a toothpaste over-squeeze, not in, not out,
waiting one more muscle twitch to sever
waste from the holding body.
While opaque milk-eyes stare flies down
to press fingerprints to your glass – sup from
your saucer of soul, as thick parmesan
permeates this dining room of road, in real death
you lay empty ...

... Unlike the beautiful Bastet – Egyptian cat
goddess, perched before your feline mystique,
gold adorned ears hold the ancients' secrets.
No domestic servant working for feed,
when you died mummified aloofness made you
mythology; there you sit carved in stone,
mocking the afterlife.

Between Coffee
& Stripping Meat

We were young men that year, that hour,
and then Liam bolted into the cool room
eyes wide, mouth pelting spittle as words
sprang from his throat ... that was the day
Liam watched his mate drift with current,
snag the bottom, disappear.
And so, we thumped to the bank, eyes stripped
every glitch, every ripple, and then a glimmer
snatched my eye and for the first time I knew
death as a taste; a dry thumping tang,
I touched water to my chest, dived
to murkiness, the squeeze against my ribs,
swept further by the current that stole our youth
and in that glimpse I also knew, nihility.

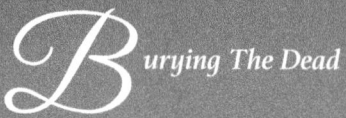

Burying The Dead

I grasped a slim candle, an hour's length,
spending wax drop by drop upon a tulip-cup,
its paper protected the parquet floor,
polished by souls searching for their Gods.

The choir's chant trembled through my bones,
no music but the music of their breath,
and their breath spoke words within the silence.
The mourning formed a subtle wave, as one
foot rocked body weight to the other foot.

My candle, burnt to its wick, murmured smoke
past my face, a lover's touch felt before
skin brushes skin. And in candle-death,
reflected opaque flesh of an empty man
caressed with coffin walls, his stillness centred.

A pebble thrown to rippled water,
The pond reverberating the fallen stone.

Your Photographic Title Read:
Alice Springs, 1885

Arrernte woman with your blackness colouring
this monochrome still – liquorice to paper
to retina, how your face warms the smile
you gush, like cloth wrapped across
your cantaloupe breasts – what is underneath
spills out, and your toothless gap – a story
I will not know – but the child you hold
in its sedge mat, lays fist clenched
– she knows your truths, and the man
who carefully placed you beneath the dappled tree,
with the hint of sun glinting against your oiled skin,
with the musty dust rubbed thick to your soles
– he knows: you will not ever die.

eirdre; Eighty-Three & Demented Down

Old woman Dierdre smears lipstick
on her lizard lips, red strips of flesh
– make her face mean but she's not
hard like her skin, just rubbed with years.
She squashes a dash of lippy against her
cheeks, makes small Jonathans each apple,
says it's easier than tweaking,
but the pretty boys don't come anymore.

Deirdre wanders down the local aisle,
stumbles across the cosmetic stand;
walls of pink, shades of brown scream
like boiled lollies when she was a child.
Her liver-speckled claws wrap knuckle-white
around a dawdling girl, Deirdre begs
the female's advice; says she's searching
new colours for a friend. Deirdre lies.

Old woman Dierdre dresses her locks
with calico rags, scrunches them into her
pillow and rolls with sleep, dreams musk
men who whisper hot breath and smother
thick hands. Deirdre wakes drenched
with scattered memories, reaches
the hand-mirror – rubs arthritis
... against her youth.

Hurtling

    The stranger's trunk *thuds*
the bonnet, ricochets the windscreen,
   as a wallaby at dusk might *whack*
   the death of country, alone, pale.
    His forearms splay, claw wipers,
     like a man who's buried alive
   claws the coffin walls, scratching
    for breath, writing his epitaph:
        ... *Death by Taxi.*

   And the cab idling by the curb
   half-cocked searching the next
    dullard to step across its view,

while inside the man of secrets runs
    his finger-comb through hair,
   brushes shards off, his navy suit
  beyond glass, as a fireman would
  wear his to rub against the flame,
  tosses five bucks to the empty seat,
     and hails another cab.

 Passing Through

She passed her gifts past her daughter
into her daughter's daughter's hands.
The amassed largesses, gestures
from the dying woman cheating the instance
of death, whose need to share her past,
her belongings, left her ego occupying space
on someone else's shelf.

But in the echo of clinked crystal, memories
of gifts received pass mellowed with time, clasped
within the palm of her daughter's daughter,
the old woman lingers, always passing
past her daughter and into someone else's arms.

 sleep

    She lays her whispered words across the sheets
     like crisp paper collecting ink, her tears blur
then sink into cotton – she is Astrid of the flannel.
      And he with acrid words that rip her skin,
    bunt her to the other side, his sleep sublime
    … his love smoulders dark, as the moon
       murmurs to his masculine breath.

Astrid's reach is for his hand, but the one who feels
her shudder, reels to the touch, and she falls, sullen
  into furrowed sheets till dawn nibbles the night,
and the ribald morning annuls their wedded sleep.

Mourning – Before Time

He ushered, with years of palms across my back,
toward his satchel; the tan leather, scuffed-white
work bag, that he copper-wire stitched worn edges
with, the same wire woven through countless
armatures, like baskets intricate with cane,
coppering the insides of motors, a monotone
tapestry, on weekends, for overtime – we never saw.

He unfurled the bankbook, put aside for death,
and there in numbers, to match those years
rubbed a muscle twitch devoid of sentiment;
his demands for mahogany.
His words thrust across my face, this stranger's
exchange like a passing handshake, or oil smeared
across his dirt rag, that I should soak in wonder.

He draws me into old rooms like metal ductiled
into thin wire, he weaves my childhood in a mix
of cashmere bouquet and glycerine but still
his nails scream to be cut, released, like filament
bits that tumble from his vise, and so
I practise this cortège – two steps behind.
Waiting.
Waiting.

Secrets Soaked In Wood

She gathers her words from walls,
incomplete memories, mere echoes
collapsing over themselves, unfolds
too late, her walls won't speak.
The limed-boards stand rampart,
wolf her drones, she chisels screams
into grain. Her quarrel loaded
with dreams and gilt-edged men.
But deaf with darkness, she rhymes
like flint, promises inner fire
only finds she's stranded with vowels
abandoned by ears, she drifts
like music for the dead, weeps
against tear-soaked wood
and lines her room with secrets.

He Knew A Woman, Years Ago

She brandished males as Summer prickles
ravish burnt, thirsty grass,
carried eyes deep with warmth,
burst pear-tears over fine laugh lines.
He knew to hold her thought,
run memory along those times,
sent cotton-pressed nipples erect,
as his fingers itched to touch.
His flesh throbbed to wrap limb with limb,
held his wispy-fabric gaze,
let his mind massage her thighs,
naked legs down to a heart tattoo
centred red, on the inside left ankle,
a kiss smacked on skin.

Her heart hinted forward suggestions
but delivered less, mere love-bites
fading yellow after lust died.
A woman, whose blonde eased
dark roots, adorned like a gift
wrapped in second-hand paper,
takes the edge off the surprise.
A woman, whose wardrobe now boasts
foreign suits and stylish scarves,
yet he still can't see – past her disguise.

Time Comes To Leave

The other day, my mother edified a tale
relayed to her, from friends of friends
about a man and wife: *brimmed with smite*
the lady grasped a cleave, held the silver
blade to her husband's throat, he woke to words
so shrill they left no choice; she'd run it through
unless he left that night, so he went,
the story goes.

And then my mother related another
about some other wife who recounted
this parable to her other half, as he rolled
in their bed of hate. And within the time
that's captured to whisper this again,
grabbed the hint, detached himself, so ended
their married life.

… And with a strangled laugh my own departs
for work, and imparts a similar allegory, to me.

 ove-Dead Bouquet

Splayed at the base of her heart
shaped stone – engraving death,
the desiccated rust-faded rose
once cream and flesh – fragrant
as a wisp of her mother's scent
no longer lingers on the breeze
but grinds against iron-tinged clay,
outback red – not cemetery pristine.
The stillborn, dated 1975
and titled: *Sleeping Peacefully*
in tombstone manuscript
mason-carved years ago,
and just as neglected, or disavowed,
does not sleep ...

She died sometime between
conception and natal birth –
albeit there is/was ... no life,
just denial, and an unkempt grave.
The dehydrated garland – an offering
appeasing God, but there are so many
deities buried here ... their sacrifice
already taken, symbolic as time.

Grounded For Life

I grasped my plane ticket,
as your voice echoed my mind,
how you begged me to stay
... *one night*, step the threshold
of your life, to ripple flesh
along my spine, meld our sweat.

That night our first child spored,
she grew as fungi in the dark, silent,
drew from me more than warmth,
kept me grounded, for life.

Intensive Care

One splattered man-frog iodine drenched
and drunk, charms the white-coats with half-jokes
and conquered flies. His slashed neck-dissection
is discreetly covered.
A window view blasts white to opiate
affected bug-eyes, restless, he grabs black
Ray-Bans, this floor, dark opium dens too hard
to find ... pity the glassless rest.
Splayed across the patient-white bed, pinned
like a specimen, a mini-beast. Drug dazed
he pulses blood, races pressure machines
to chase green beeps and score, then disappear.
The crimson stained catheter and saline drip
hang from hooks like ripe fruit juice-packed
before they're plucked.
The man-frog spills his guts.
Half dead, half alive his gaze but morphine
clouds his sight, instead he falls between
Neptune and Pluto, dreams fused bones,
filleted skin and serial killers stitching seams.

He's an embroidered sampler, not for wooden frames
... flesh canvas – Surgeon's art.

Her Stomach Breaks Out

As Ruby's sweat bleeds against cotton sheets
she dreams of theatres once danced across
... of a time dealt with in increments
of whim and trailed in gold chiffon.

Her muscled-limbs precision placed
on musty boards, rank, and raked for sight
not *pirouettes*. Ruby sweeps fingertips across
oak balustrades, snatches splinters
against the dark to offset the bite
of throbs and aches, with a swift flick
she grease-paints her eyes and lips
with more care than she unfolds to a child.

Her mind partners her soul,
her stomach explodes mid *arabesque*.
And as she lies entwined in lover's breath
Ruby holds the holes with her balletic hands.

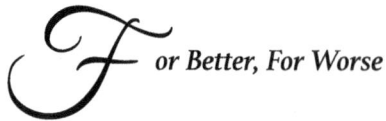 or Better, For Worse

The dead hour comes ...
I watch my pupils dilate to the edge
of climax as the gentle titian gel-caps fuzz
me heavy, thick. I open the bathroom
cabinet and clasp the small marble cache
of gold rings and marquee-cut diamonds
I haven't worn in years ...

Years of thickening fingers
like tender trunks wrapping yet another
layer of growth around its stump – mark
the rings of time to be cut clean through
one day as some stranger will count the days
... this is the year the winds blew hard,
and this here, this swirl of a knot – this was
the year she gave and gave but got nothing back.
And those little gel-caps will numb the bending
of the green stalk before it does not bend back.

THE GREY BETWEEN

I wear those rings past the first tip, pressed white
before the knuckles – but long to be that slender
sapling lifted by breeze as though I would never fall.
But the dead hour knocks and I pluck a little grey
lash from the black sparseness that surrounds
those pupils that see me for who I'd like to be.
I cannot fit those rings. I cannot reflect accurately
from the glass. I cannot know how I am perceived.
I do not know the correct colour of my blood,
but each day as I enter my husband's house
I bleed without shedding a drop.

s & Them

Becalmed little souls percolate
jocular granules of lunacy
in their intrigue as we slide on
this blood-warm day, past
the bone-white high-rises of old
stone divided by green and new
graves – brown mounds of fresh
death, they tease: *hold your breath*
but whisper tortuously inside:
I'm not ready yet, and later,
when the lattice of night unfurls
they chant again to the ancients
to absolve their sins, lulling
themselves to practiced sleep.

As we, skeletal structures
swathed in flesh, sit as creatures
encapsulated in metal shells,
caress the blackened path,
as moored voices in the back beseech:
what is beyond, what is beyond?
We dream echoes coffin-boxed
and bleat forgiveness.
… But what do the dead ask for
when everything has been said?

ABOUT NADINE ELLIS

Nadine Ellis is an Australian poet, writing about everyday life: focusing on family dynamics, motherhood, imploding relationships, emotional damage, through to death and the wake left behind. She writes as a cathartic release – processing life's experiences – spilling out her internal thoughts – with hope that her words touch others, to let them know they are not alone.

Nadine was born in South Australia to Eastern European parents. She is a mother to four adult daughters, and is a Radiographer, who has worked as an Academic teaching into Medical Radiations at the University of South Australia for the last twelve years.

Nadine's poetry has previously appeared in America, and throughout Australia, within literary journals, and poetry anthologies. The Grey Between is Nadine Ellis' first book of collected poems.

CONNECT WITH NADINE

If you would like to connect with Nadine Ellis please go to nadineellis.com and sign up.

Nadine Ellis official website:

www.ingramcontent.com/pod-product-compliance
Lightning Source LLC
Chambersburg PA
CBHW061729070526
44583CB00024B/3064